ENDOP

Throughout the New Testament, whenever the people of God boldly proclaim the gospel, a bold response from heaven comes to bring breakthrough. In *Decrees that Unlock Heaven's Power*, Tommy and Miriam Evans empower each one of us to confidently declare the truth of God's Word, inviting the breakthroughs that have been promised to happen once again. Faith-filled proclamations seed the cloud that releases the rains of heaven over our lives. I encourage you to read each of these daily devotionals with great anticipation. There is genuine power in our declarations, as nothing happens in the kingdom until something is spoken.

—**Bill Johnson**
Bethel Church
Redding, California
Author of *The Mind of God* and *Born for Significance*

As I read Tommy and Miriam's devotional book, the thought that was the most prevalent to me was, "This is a life-changing book!" Not only is it daily bread, but it is full of revelation that will transform your life!

—**Cindy Jacobs**
Generals International

My dad, Zig Ziglar, was committed to the concept of positive self-talk. He used it, taught it, created self-talk materials, and infused all within his sphere of influence with its benefits. If your heart's desire is to serve Christ and others while enriching your own life, *Decrees that Unlock Heaven's Power* is just the tool to help you achieve that goal.

—**Tom Ziglar**
Author and proud son of Zig Ziglar

Decrees that Unlock Heaven's Power extracts the words of truth found throughout the Bible in a very practical but profound way that will have the power to break strongholds in our lives. As we begin to speak these promises, the Lord will richly dwell in the intricate details of who we are. These declarations will transform us beyond a place of mere living and catapult us into fulfilling our destiny. Tommy and Miriam's reckless love for God leads us to a place of incredible vulnerability, dependence, and confidence in our Savior. Read on and discover that in Christ we find our meaning, joy, and fulfillment.

—**Dr. Karla Evans**
Clinical Psychologist
Co-founder of Anticipate Joy

Tommy and Miriam Evans are the original, anointed power couple who move in the divine nature of God's favor, power, and joy. They release an open heaven wherever they go igniting signs, wonders, and miracles. The presence of God flows freely through them to break generational curses and words of knowledge and the prophetic unction reveals the matters of the heart. Out of their vast experiences as revivalists and numerous spiritual, healing encounters they have put together this incredible forty-day devotional that will transform your personal life, empowering you to become a faith-filled, fiery Kingdom minister. Learn how to decree the Word of God to release an expectant hope, move in the gifts of the Spirit, and learn Kingdom warfare as a glory carrier of the Holy Spirit. This revolutionary book, *Decrees that Unlock Heaven's Power,* will generously baptize you in a new level of love, wisdom, and authority causing you to become a shining one who carries God's glory!

—**Dr. Barbie L. Breathitt**
Bestselling Author
Breath of the Spirit Ministries

Decrees that Unlock Heaven's Power is a book that every believer should read, because it calls us to partner with God and believe in His promises for us. *Decrees that Unlock Heaven's Power* has been such a blessing to me because it is so theologically rich and so intensely practical! These daily readings are fire to the heart and soul. *Decrees that Unlock Heaven's Power* is a source of spiritual downloads and personal growth that speaks life into all generations, as God's promises come alive through our decrees and declarations. I believe that God hears our fervent prayers and declarations, and He invites us to partner with Heaven and declare His words over us. Each page conveys the heart of Jesus and His power and love for each and every one of us.

—**Ayelen Saavedra**
Global Prophetic Ministry
Associate Minister of Trinity Church
Author of *Manual of Evangelism*

As we face uncertain seasons, powerful spiritual infusions from heaven seem essential. Tommy and Miriam Evans provide scriptural insight, life experience, and prophetic edge through these daily encounters. Their short but pointed devotions encourage our hearts by giving clarity and hope. Your daily visit with Tommy and Miriam is sure to result in a deeper experience with Jesus and a more wonder-filled love journey of faith! Thank you Tommy and Miriam for this much-needed boost to our soul!

—Jim Hennesy
Senior Pastor, Trinity Church
Cedar Hill, Texas

We all want to be victorious followers of Christ used in miracles, signs, and wonders, but many of us do not know where to begin or how to grow the gifts of the Spirit. Tommy and Miriam Evans give us a tool to become effective and powerful in the Kingdom of God. We use faith-filled words to declare the promises of God into the broken places and situations in our lives, our cities, the nation, and the world. I am excited to prayer-walk/run my city carrying *Decrees that Unlock Heaven's Power* with me. Our words can create life and this book has done the hard work for us.

Now we can attach great faith to the declaration of God's words. I have already begun using the declarations and can sense my faith growing. Thank you Tommy and Miriam!

—Becky Hennesy
Co-Senior Pastor, Trinity Church
Cedar Hill, Texas

Decrees that Unlock

HEAVEN'S POWER

FOR MIRACLES

Decrees that Unlock

HEAVEN'S POWER

FOR MIRACLES

*40 Prayers and Declarations that Release Miracles,
Breakthrough, and Supernatural Answers*

Tommy & Miriam Evans

DEDICATION

We dedicate this devotional to our heavenly Father. You always encourage us to believe in ourselves and go for our dreams. The journey we take with You is our highest honor and privilege. We love You deeply.

ACKNOWLEDGMENTS

We want to say a big thank you to our beautiful and loving children. Your love, joy, and kindness fill our heart in a deep way. We are honored to do life with you, and it is our highest privilege to call you our own. Baby bears, we love you.

We also want to say thank you to our extended family. Your love and prayers got us through some of the toughest times as well as some of the most rewarding. Thank you all for being voices of encouragement to us. We love you all.

A special thank you to so many of our fathers and mothers in the faith: Jim and Becky Hennesy, Mike and Cindy Jacobs, Bill and Beni Johnson, Dan and Marti Duke, Stan and Deanna Jones, Deborah Coombs, and Randy Clark for pouring into us and encouraging us to always believe for more of God. You all have played such monumental roles in our lives, and we are eternally grateful.

We want to especially thank all our past and present students. Your hunger and passion for Jesus ignites our hearts and keeps us pressing forward. We love you.

Finally, thank you to our Trinity Church family. We are so honored to help pastor all of you. Your love, worship, and commitment to Jesus make pastoring altogether worth it.

DESTINY IMAGE® PUBLISHERS, INC.
P.O. Box 310, Shippensburg, PA 17257-0310
"Promoting Inspired Lives."

This book and all other Destiny Image and Destiny Image Fiction books are available at Christian bookstores and distributors worldwide.

Cover design by Eileen Rockwell

For more information on foreign distributors, call 717-532-3040.

Reach us on the Internet: www.destinyimage.com.

ISBN 13 TP: 978-0-7684-6011-7

ISBN 13 eBook: 978-0-7684-6012-4

For Worldwide Distribution, Printed in the U.S.A.

1 2 3 4 5 6 7 8 / 25 24 23 22 21

Contents

Foreword

The book you are about to read is unique. While there are many excellent devotional books, *Decrees that Unlock Heaven's Power* by Tommy and Miriam Evans is about you connecting to God and being used to release God's power in the earth both on a personal and corporate level. It is about decreeing.

I have been privileged to get to know the authors on a personal level over the past few years. They live what they write about, each and every day. They start right off with the important theme of renewing your mind linking with the fact that God wants to do exceedingly abundantly above what we ask or think.

The basic premise throughout the over 200 decrees is that faith comes by hearing and hearing by the word of

God (see Rom. 10:17). I learned these principles under a great teacher of faith, Dr. Frederick Price. Prior to this time, I was very southern in my culture and said many things out of my mouth that were contrary to releasing power and faith. Things such as, "Oh, honey, I am just so worried about you!" Another was, "That just scares me to death!" Somehow if you worried enough about someone, which isn't biblical, or something scared you, you were proving that you really cared about what was happening. I have to admit, at times those things still slip out of my mouth.

What is my point? In some ways, we are trained to release negative rather than positive declarations over our lives. Job 22:28 says, "You will also declare a thing, and it will be established for you; so light will shine on your ways."

Many years ago I was part of a church that was amazing in many ways, but we were taught that everything we prayed should have a, "If it be Your will," tacked onto the end of it.

Tommy and Miriam have written a book full of decrees with the revealed will of God that will transform your thinking and your life! Decrees such as, "The anointing on my life destroys every yoke of oppression, bondage, affliction, and disease in my life and those to whom I minister." Absolutely powerful! Just take a minute and say that out loud. I just did and I could feel the presence of God and faith rise up in my heart when I did so.

Tommy and Miriam live an overcoming life. They have five children, they pastor, and they have a mentorship group that they meet with on a regular basis. Even though they live a full and busy life, they live what they have written in these pages. On a regular basis, they are seeing signs and wonders and miracles. God wants you to walk in power and miracles. The same Holy Spirit who lives in them lives in you!

Many prophets and ministers around the world are prophesying that we are moving into the greatest awakening and revival the world has ever known. This very well could be the end-time harvest that we knew would come one day. That means we are all getting closer and closer to stepping over to glory. It could be a century or ten years yet. God wants to come back for a triumphant church that has been transformational in the earth. We all need the "how-tos" to have lived up to our full potential.

Do yourself a favor and apply these decrees to your life on a daily basis. You will find that you will be able to overcome sorrow, financial defeat, sickness, and other oppressions of the enemy as well as change the lives of others who need a miracle. God's word is alive and powerful! (See Hebrews 4:12.)

You are on an exciting journey to be an overcomer!

Many rich blessings!

—Cindy Jacobs
Generals International
Dallas, Texas

Introduction

In our book, *Decree's that Unlock Heaven's Power,* we have the wonderful opportunity to share a life-changing journey with you. We believe that this devotional will help you will discover the power of declarations. Daily declarations have changed everything for us. Once we realized the biblical principle of speaking over our destinies, we began to partner with what God says about us in His Word by making declarations ourselves. As we did this, we noticed a dramatic shift. A positive change took place in our earthly perspectives, one that unlocked heaven's power over our lives. Worldly circumstances no longer limited heaven's activity over our lives (see Col. 3:2). The shift came from within us. We believe that declaring biblical truths over your life will release the power of transformation.

This powerful transformation is the result of some fascinating keys found in scripture. We believe Romans 12:2 is one of those keys: "Be transformed by the renewing of your mind." According to scripture, this is the first step to discerning God's will for our lives. Transformation begins with the way we think, and how we think influences the way we speak. Luke 6:45 says, "For out of the abundance of the heart his mouth speaks." The words we speak flow from what we believe. What we believe affects the words we speak, thus creating an interesting ellipse. Our thoughts and words work so closely together it is sometimes difficult to decipher which influence comes first. For that reason, the Bible tells us that we must guard our hearts because our heart's status effects life issues (see Prov. 4:23). It may be safe to conclude our thought life determines who we are and the decisions we make.

The Hebrew word for "heart" is *levav,* which includes thoughts, will, discernment, and affections. Proverbs 23:7 tells us that as a man believes in his heart, so is he.

In addition to biblical truths, secular society has recognized the connection between thoughts and behavior. The 19th century writer Ralph Waldo Emerson said, "A man is what he thinks about all day long." British philosopher and author James Allen wrote, "You are today where your thoughts take you." A recent neuroscience experiment discovered the power of our thoughts and words. Their study proved that painful or negative comments spoken or heard increased "Implicit Processing" (IMP) in the brain. In other words, negative self-talk, whether spoken, heard, or thought, can contribute to long-term anxiety. In addition, research shows the effects of negative self-talk are impacting children in an alarming way. We owe it to ourselves and future generations to renew our minds.

Some of you may be asking the same questions we asked. How can I change the way I think? My thoughts seem cyclical and automatic! Is there a way to think positive when I am not feeling positive? We are thankful we have a good Father who helped us answer these questions. Studying the Bible helped us realize the truth concerning our thought life. We found that our thoughts began to change when we chose to speak positively, regardless of our feelings. Speaking what God says about us is a game-changer. Declaring God's truth, despite life's circumstances, changes everything. Jesus demonstrates this beautifully in the gospel of Luke.

In Luke 4, we find a powerful story telling when Jesus made a public declaration of what the Father said about Him. In the synagogue on the Sabbath, Jesus picked up the scroll of Isaiah 61 and read aloud a prophecy about the coming Messiah. Jesus knew He was reading a prophecy about Himself among the people of His hometown. This story demonstrates the power of declaration. The people who were all too familiar with this carpenter's son were stunned at the words Jesus spoke, as great authority shifted the atmosphere. He did not wait for people to recognize He was the son of God before He declared who He was. Therefore, Jesus powerfully declared, "The Spirit of the Lord is upon me, and he has anointed me to be hope for the poor, healing for the brokenhearted, and new eyes for the blind, and to preach to prisoners, 'You are set free!'" (Luke 4:18 TPT).

In Luke 4, we read that Jesus made this declaration after a defining moment in the wilderness. Jesus knew His identity amid the trial. He came out of the wilderness "armed with the Holy Spirit's power" (Luke 4:14 TPT). Upon leaving the wilderness, the Holy Spirit led Jesus to His hometown synagogue to speak His identity audibly. Jesus declared what the heavenly Father said about Him through the prophet Isaiah. Isaiah's prophecy, found in Isaiah 61, was spoken hundreds of years before this moment took place. Luke 4:21 says that Jesus concluded his public declaration of Isaiah 61 by saying, "Today this Scripture is fulfilled in your hearing."

Through the prophet Isaiah, God made a promise of the coming Messiah, His Son, Jesus Christ. As Jesus declared this promise, God fulfilled the promise. When we declare God's promises over our lives, we create a partnership with God to see these promises fulfilled. When we speak God's promises, we create a sound of completion. Genesis 1 says that when God spoke, "Let there be light," all chaotic circumstances came into order. We see a fulfillment of miracles throughout scripture as Jesus spoke. Like Jesus, we can shape our future with our words. Jesus is and always will be the perfect prototype for humanity. Throughout the Bible, Jesus declared the Father's words to see a fulfillment. It would behoove us to do the same.

May you be filled with the Holy Spirit as you daily read and declare God's Word over your life. May you be empowered to believe what God says about you. May this devotional be a catalyst to unlock heaven's power over your life. May every promise be fulfilled in your hearing.

Much Love and Joy,
Tommy and Miriam Evans

Biblical Basis
for This Devotional

And do not be conformed to this world, **but be transformed by the renewing of your mind***, that you may prove what is that good and acceptable and perfect will of God* (Romans 12:2).

Now to Him who is able to do exceedingly abundantly above all that we ask or think, **according to the power that works in us***, to Him be glory in the church by Christ Jesus to all generations, forever and ever. Amen* (Ephesians 3:20).

So then faith comes by hearing, and hearing by the word of God (Romans 10:17).

You will also declare a thing, and it will be established for; so light will shine on your ways (Job 22:28).

You are what you are and where you are because of what has gone into your mind. You can change what you are and where you are by changing what goes into your mind.

—Zig Ziglar

Being a Revivalist

What God Says About You:

And as you go, preach this message: "Heaven's kingdom realm is accessible, close enough to touch." You must continually bring healing to lepers and to those who are sick, and make it your habit to break off the demonic presence from people, and raise the dead back to life. Freely you have received the power of the kingdom, so freely release it to others (Matthew 10:7-8 TPT).

Author's Note:

Did you know that you were not only born to be intimate with God, but you were also born to change the world? A revivalist is one who has been commissioned by Christ to extend His kingdom by bringing the good news of the kingdom and releasing divine encounters to others. As a revivalist, you become a carrier of a heavenly atmosphere that awakens and revives people to an awareness of the power and presence of God. You were born to be a revivalist! Now activate this truth by speaking these declarations over your life. Much Love!

Declarations:

Matthew 10:7, Acts 1:8, Acts 10:38, Mark 16:15-18

"I am a revivalist, and everywhere I go people are revived and awakened to the empowering presence of Jesus."

"I consistently bring God encounters to my family and others."

> "Signs, wonders, and miracles follow me because I believe. I choose today to release to others what I have been given so lives can be changed and God's kingdom advanced."

"Like Jesus and the apostles, I am a revivalist. People, cities, and nations are impacted because of what I carry."

"I decree that the anointing on my life as a revivalist brings healing and deliverance to those in need."

"People are renewed and refreshed by the Manifest Presence in and on my life."

Prayer:

"Lord, thank You for Your promises over me. Thank You for choosing me to go and bear much fruit for Your name's sake. Lord, I agree according to Your Word that I am a revivalist commissioned by You to bring revival and awakening to a lost and dying world. Amen."

2

Being Anointed

What God Says About You:

The Spirit of the Lord is upon me, and he has anointed me to be hope for the poor, healing for the brokenhearted, and new eyes for the blind, and to preach to prisoners, "You are set free!" (Luke 4:18-19 TPT)

But you have an anointing from the Holy One, and you know all things (1 John 2:20).

Author's Note:

The biblical word "anointed" in Greek is *chrio,* which means to be consecrated or set apart for a work of service. Another meaning for the word *chrio* is to be smeared with

---

oil. In other words, as believers, we become smeared with the oil of God's presence and our work of service is to proclaim the good news of the gospel, to heal the sick, and to set the oppressed free! You are anointed by the Holy Spirit! Now activate this truth by speaking these declarations over your life. Much Love!

Declarations:

Luke 4:18-19, 1 John 2:20, Acts 10:38,
Acts 1:8, Psalm 92:10, Isaiah 10:27

"Like Jesus, I am anointed to heal the sick, to raise the dead, to set the oppressed free, and proclaim the good news of the kingdom."

"God anoints me daily with the fresh oil of His presence, making me strong and empowering my life to be victorious in every situation."

> "The anointing on my life sets me apart to love like Jesus loved, to walk like Jesus walked, and to give like Jesus gave."

"The anointing on my life destroys every yoke of oppression, bondage, affliction, and disease in my life and those to whom I minister."

"The anointing of the Holy Spirit within me teaches me all things."

Prayer:

"Lord, thank You for anointing me with the oil of Your presence. Thank You that Your anointing destroys the yoke of bondage, sickness, and disease on me and others. I agree with Your word that I am anointed. Amen."

3

WALKING IN THE MIRACULOUS

What God Says About You:

And these miraculous signs will accompany those who believe: They will drive out demons in the power of my name. They will speak in tongues. They will be supernaturally protected from snakes and from drinking anything poisonous. And they will lay hands on the sick and heal them (Mark 16:17-18 TPT).

Author's Note:

Did you know that Jesus lived a miracle life? His whole life was a miracle! Jesus said, "*As the Father has sent Me, I also send you*" (John 20:21). That's great news! Jesus has sent you and me to live a life of the miraculous! Now is the time for you to step into the fullness of your inheritance! Now activate this truth by speaking these declarations over your life. Much Love!

Declarations:

Mark 16:17-18, Matthew 10:7-8,
Acts 5:12, Acts 19:11-12

"Because I believe in Jesus, I live a life of the miraculous with signs and wonders following me."

"Like Jesus, I live a miracle life."

"God releases a flow of extraordinary miracles through my hands, through my words, and through my life."

> "When I see an impossible situation, I run to it, knowing that God will bring about a miracle."

"Creative miracles are a normal occurrence for me because I am a child of God."

"Miracles are normal for me in Jesus' name!"

Prayer:

"Lord, I am so grateful that You would choose me to live a life of the miraculous. May every miracle in my life bring glory and honor to Your name. Amen."

4

DIVINE HEALING
FOR YOURSELF

What God Says About You:

For I am the Lord who heals you
(Exodus 15:26).

He sent His word and healed them
(Psalm 107:20).

And by His stripes we are healed
(Isaiah 53:5).

Author's Note:

Did you know that Jesus died on the cross not only for
your eternal salvation, but also for your deliverance and

divine healing? The biblical word for salvation is *sozo*, which means healed, saved, and delivered. Jesus paid a price so you can be healed! According to the Bible it is one hundred percent God's will for you to walk in divine health. Divine healing is your inheritance! Now activate this truth by speaking these declarations over your life. Much Love!

Declarations:

Exodus 15:16, Psalm 107:20, Isaiah 53:5,
Acts 10:38, Luke 5:13, Romans 8:11, Luke 4:40

"Because Jesus healed everyone who came to Him, I come to Him and choose today to walk in divine health by the power of His name."

"I speak to my body and command it to line up according to the order of God's will that I am healed by the stripes of Jesus."

> "Because Jesus went to the cross for my healing, I declare that I am healed."

"Sickness, pain, and disease have *no* authority over my body, in Jesus' name."

"The spirit of resurrection power lives in me and brings life to my mortal being."

"You sent forth Your Word for me so that I can now stand in perfect health."

Prayer:

> "Lord, thank You for Your healing power. I believe that You died on the cross not only for my salvation, but also my healing. I agree that I am healed in Jesus' name according to Your word. Amen."

RELEASING HEALING POWER

What God Says About You:

Empower us, as your servants, to speak the word of God freely and courageously. Stretch out your hand of power through us to heal, and to move in signs and wonders by the name of your holy Son, Jesus! (Acts 4:29-30 TPT)

Jesus repeated his greeting, "Peace to you!" And he told them, "Just as the Father has sent me, I'm now sending you (John 20:21 TPT).

And these signs will follow those who believe: In My name they will cast out demons; they will speak with new tongues; they will take up serpents; and if they drink anything deadly, it will by no means hurt them; they will lay hands on the sick, and they will recover (Mark 16:17-18).

Author's Note:

According to the Bible, you carry healing power! Christ has not only given you authority and permission to lay hands on the sick, but He has given each one of us a mandate to heal in His name. There is healing power in your hands and in your mouth! Now activate this truth by speaking these declarations over your life. Much Love!

Declarations:

Acts 4:29-30, Acts 4:12-16, Matthew 10:7-8, Mark 16:17-18, Matthew 4:23-24, Luke 4:40, Acts 10:38, James 5:15

"Like Jesus, I am anointed with the Holy Spirit. I choose today to do good by healing the sick and setting free those who are oppressed by the devil because God is with me."

"I have been commissioned by Jesus to heal the sick and cast out demons."

> "When I lay hands on the sick, they will recover in Jesus' name."

"My hands and my words carry healing power."

"Because Jesus lives inside me, I have authority to release healing to my family, friends, and community."

Prayer:

"Lord, thank You for anointing me with Your Spirit to bring healing to others. May the healing power of Jesus be displayed in my life and bring You glory in the earth. Amen."

6

RELEASING PRAYERS OF POWER

What God Says About You:

For tremendous power is released through the passionate, heartfelt prayer of a godly believer! (James 5:16 TPT)

You will also declare a thing, and it will be established for you; so light will shine on your ways (Job 22:28).

Author's Note:

Your prayers carry creative power! Jesus gave His disciples a prayer model that includes, "On earth as it is in heaven" (Matthew 6:10). Heaven is our focus for all prayer. We are asking God's world to invade ours according to the order of heaven. We believe today that as you open your heart to these truths you will be activated to a new level of power in your personal prayer life. Now activate this truth by speaking these declarations over your life. Much Love!

Declarations:

James 5:16, Job 20:28, John 15:16,
Ephesians 2:6, Mark 11:26

"Because I have been given a seat of power in the heavenly realm through Christ, my prayers are powerful and effective."

"Today I believe as I pray according to Your will, I will receive what I am asking for."

"When I pray, the kingdom is unlocked, and heaven is opened to invade impossible situations, turning things around for my good and those I love in Jesus' name."

> "I know in my heart that God hears my prayers, and He will answer me."

"My prayers release the kingdom and declare God's perfect will in the earth."

Prayer:

> "Lord Jesus, thank You for giving up Your life so that I have access to pray and commune with You. I love You so much. Amen."

7

GOD'S PROMISES

What God Says About You:

There has not failed one word of all [God's] *good promise* (1 Kings 8:56).

Not one promise from God is empty of power. Nothing is impossible with God! (Luke 1:37 TPT)

Author's Note:

Wow! What powerful promises are found in God's Word! When God gives us a promise it never fails! Every promise God has made to us carries fulfillment power! Get ready to receive your promise! Now activate this truth by speaking these declarations over your life. Much Love!

Declarations:

Ephesians 3:20, 1 Kings 8:56, Luke 1:37,
Numbers 23:19, Psalm 119:89

"I trust all of Your promises for me because there is divine power in them to be fulfilled."

"Every promise You have ever made to me will be fulfilled in my life and in the lives of those I love, in Jesus' name."

"As I hold on to what is true, I give myself permission to exaggerate Your goodness over me because I know You are faithful."

"You are the Lord who exceeds my wildest imagination and fulfills my wildest dreams. Today I declare that I am one step closer to my dreams being realized beyond imagination!"

"Nothing is impossible with God; therefore, I will see my promises come to pass."

Prayer:

"Lord, thank You that You truly are the God of promises. I make a promise to You that today I will eagerly anticipate Your goodness being made manifest. I love You, Lord. Amen."

8

GOD ENCOUNTERS

What God Says About You:

I will pour out My Spirit on all flesh; your sons and your daughters shall prophesy, your old men shall dream dreams, your young men shall see visions (Joel 2:28).

Then suddenly, after I wrote down these messages, I saw a portal open into the heavenly realm, and the same trumpet-voice I heard speaking with me at the beginning said, "Ascend into this realm! I want to reveal to you what must happen after this (Revelation 4:1 TPT).

Author's Note:

Did you know that by design you were engineered to encounter God? God encounters are part of your inheritance as a believer! The Bible was not given to us just to make us smarter and brighter. The reason the Bible has been given to us was to lead us into a divine encounter with its Author! Jesus wants you to encounter Him! This is the good news of the kingdom! Now activate this truth by speaking these declarations over your life. Much Love!

Declarations:

Joel 2:28, Habakkuk 2:2-3, Amos 3:7,
Numbers 12:6, 2 Corinthians 12:4,
1 Corinthians 2:10, Revelation 4;1-2,
Matthew 17, Book of Acts

"I consistently have dreams, visions, and prophetic encounters."

> "Heavenly encounters, angelic visitations, and spiritual happenings are normal to me and are part of my inheritance as a child of God."

"Like Jesus and His disciples, I carry an open heaven where angels ascend and descend on my life carrying fresh revelation, strength, and assignments."

"The Holy Spirit is my guide with all heavenly encounters and teaches me how to navigate through them."

Prayer:

"Thank You, Holy Spirit, that You search the deepest mysteries of God and make them known to me. Lord, I choose today to step into divine encounters through faith. I am so thankful that I have the privilege to discover all that You have for me. I love You. Amen"

9

LIVING IN CONTAGIOUS JOY

What God Says About You:

For the kingdom of God is not a matter of rules about food and drink, but is in the realm of the Holy Spirit, filled with righteousness, peace, and joy (Romans 14:17 TPT).

In Your presence there is fullness of joy; at Your right hand are pleasures forevermore (Psalm 16:11).

He who sits in the heavens shall laugh (Psalm 2:4).

Author's Note:

According to Romans 14:17, joy is one third of the kingdom! When my children were babies, any time I would reach down and get in their face they would always smile. In the Bible, the meaning for the word *presence* is "face." So when Psalm 16:11 states, "in Your presence is fullness of joy," it's saying, "In God's *face* there is fullness of joy." When we get in our heavenly Father's face, it puts a smile on ours! Now activate this truth by speaking these declarations over your life. Much Love!

Declarations:

Romans, 14:17, Nehemiah 8:10, Psalm 2:4,
Hebrews 1:9, Proverbs 17:22

"Because I am filled with the Spirit of God, I am filled with contagious joy."

"I laugh hysterically at every lie of the devil because I know that God has my back!"

"Like Jesus, I am anointed with the oil of joy that is transferable to others."

> "I walk in an abundance of joy that brings healing to my entire being—spirit, soul, and body."

"Joy through laughter is a weapon that God has equipped me with for any challenge that I might face."

"I am filled today with God's joy that brings healing to my body and gladness to my heart."

Prayer:

"Lord, thank You for the gift of joy. Today I choose to let You fill me again with great joy. Amen."

10

Carrying an Open Heaven

What God Says About You:

Then he dreamed, and behold, a ladder was set up on the earth, and its top reached to heaven; and there the angels of God were ascending and descending on it (Genesis 28:12).

And [Jesus] *said to him, "Most assuredly, I say to you, hereafter you shall see heaven open, and the angels of God ascending and descending upon the Son of Man"* (John 1:51).

So Jesus said to them again, "Peace to you! As the Father has sent Me, I also send you" (John 20:21).

Author's Note:

Did you know that when you received the infilling of the Holy Spirit you became an open door to the heavenly realm? You now have access to God's eternal kingdom where angels ascend and descend! This realm provides miracle power, fresh anointing, wisdom, revelation, and divine encounters. Now activate this truth by speaking these declarations over your life. Much Love!

Declarations:

Genesis 28:12, John 1:51, John 20:21,
Joel 2:28, Matthew 10:7, Revelation 4

"Like Jesus, I carry an open heaven where angels ascend and descend upon my life with fresh anointing, new assignments, and divine help to advance the kingdom of God."

"The open heaven that I carry shifts the atmosphere over people, cities, and nations."

> "When people come into my atmosphere, they come under the influence of the Holy Spirit, encountering joy, peace, and breakthrough."

"Like the apostle Peter, the open heaven I carry has the ability to release miracle power."

Prayer:

"Lord Jesus, thank You that You passed the baton unto me to carry an open heaven for my benefit and others'. I believe that I carry an open heaven in Jesus' name. Amen."

11

THE GIFTS OF
THE SPIRIT

What God Says About You:

*Each believer is given continuous revelation by
the Holy Spirit to benefit not just himself but
all. For example: The Spirit gives to one the gift
of the word of wisdom. To another, the same
Spirit gives the gift of the word of revelation
knowledge. And to another, the same Spirit
gives the gift of faith. And to another, the same
Spirit gives gifts of healing. And to another the
power to work miracles. And to another the gift
of prophecy. And to another the gift to discern
what the Spirit is speaking. And to another the
gift of speaking different kinds of tongues. And*

to another the gift of interpretation of tongues
(1 Corinthians 12:7-11 TPT).

Author's Note:

The Holy Spirit in us wants to love the world around us. His gifts are designed to release His nature and express His heart to the believer as well as the unbeliever. God wants to activate every gift in your life and empower you to effectively use them for kingdom purposes. Now activate this truth by speaking these declarations over your life. Much Love!

Declarations:

1 Corinthians 12:8-11, 1 Corinthians 14, Book of Acts

"Like Paul the apostle, I can operate in any of the gifts of the Holy Spirit to bring God encounters to those around me."

"The gifts of faith, healing, and working of miracles operate in my life and in my mouth, releasing power to the world around me."

"Gifts of prophecy, tongues, and interpretation of tongues flow through my mouth to bring glory to God and edification to the church."

"I consistently receive wisdom, discernment, and words of knowledge that release revelation and kingdom solutions to my spheres of influence."

Prayer:

"Holy Spirit, thank You for distributing and activating Your gifts to me. Today I earnestly desire the greater gifts. Help me to continue to grow in every gift to its fullest capacity to bring You glory. Amen."

12

LIVING IN THE HOLY SPIRIT

What God Says About You:

And I will ask the Father and he will give you another Savior, the Holy Spirit of Truth, who will be to you a friend just like me—and he will never leave you. The world won't receive him because they can't see him or know him. But you know him intimately because he remains with you and will live inside you (John 14:16-17 TPT).

If the Spirit is the source of our life, we must also allow the Spirit to direct every aspect of our lives (Galatians 5:25 TPT).

Author's Note:

Did you know that because of Jesus you no longer live in your old sin nature, but you now live in the Spirit? When you received Jesus, you became one in spirit with Him. You have eternal access to His thoughts, affections, and fellowship. You have permission to enjoy a beautiful journey with the Holy Spirit! Now activate this truth by speaking these declarations over your life. Much Love!

Declarations:

1 Corinthians 6:17, Galatians 5:25,
Romans 8:9, John 14:16-17, John 7

"I believe in my heart that the Holy Spirit has come to me so that I may have intimate fellowship with Him."

"I speak to my body, soul, and spirit and say, 'You are not dominated by the flesh, but you are led by the impulses of the Holy Spirit.'"

"Today I declare that no other spirit shall rule over me but the empowering presence of the Holy Spirit."

> "Because of Jesus, I have been unified forever with the Holy Spirit who never leaves me."

"I declare that my love for the Holy Spirit grows deeper and deeper every day."

"I am a friend of the Holy Spirit. My love for Him grows deeper and wider every day."

Prayer:

"Holy Spirit, thank You for coming to be my helper, teacher, comforter, and friend. I cannot wait to spend the rest of my days with You. I love You deeply. Amen."

13

Being a Fountain of Hope

What God Says About You:

Now may God, the fountain of hope, fill you to overflowing with uncontainable joy and perfect peace as you trust in him. And may the power of the Holy Spirit continually surround your life with his super-abundance until you radiate with hope! (Romans 15:13 TPT)

Be strong and of good courage, do not fear nor be afraid of them; for the Lord your God, He is the One who goes with you. He will not leave you or forsake you (Deuteronomy 31:6).

Author's Note:

"Hope" is an expectation that something good is about to happen. The enemy of your soul wants you to be hopeless so you will not radiate hope to the world. Hope is a powerful weapon that dismantles despair and creates anticipation rooted in the goodness of God. You were born to be a hope reformer, bringing hope to the hopeless! You have been given a mandate of hope! Now activate this truth by speaking these declarations over your life. Much Love!

Declarations:

Romans 15:13, Deuteronomy 31:6, Colossians 1:17

"I declare that I am filled with uncontainable joy releasing hope to those around me."

"I am filled with perfect peace bringing resolve to chaotic situations."

> "I am a hope reformer who releases
> and imparts life by the power
> of the Holy Spirit."

"I radiate and release hope to my family, friends, and community."

"I declare that my life is surrounded with super abundance that radiates light and life to myself and others."

"Because the Lord is with me, my hope is secure and carries power to bring forth good."

Prayer:

"Lord, thank You that You have made me a fountain of hope. Your empowering presence causes me to be a hope reformer of life and truth to the world around me. Amen."

14

God's Word in Me

What God Says About Me:

Yahweh's Word is perfect in every way; how it revives our souls! Yahweh's laws lead us to truth, and his ways change the simple into wise. Yahweh's teachings are right and make us joyful; his precepts are so pure! (Psalm 19:7-8 TPT)

Author's Note:

You have been given a weapon. You have been given a promise book. You have been given a playbook that brings judgment on your enemies and a victory song to your heart. You have been given the Word of God. God's Word is not just a book of meaningless words on a page, but a book of power that carries weight. God's word truly revives us and calibrates us to hear God's voice. It awakens us to destiny and presses us into purpose. Now activate this truth by speaking these declarations over your life. Much Love!

Declarations:

Psalm 19:7, Psalm 1:1-3, Hebrews 4:12,
Isaiah 55:11, Romans 10:17, Psalm 119:105

"Your Word accomplishes everything that You intend bringing great fruitfulness in my life."

"Your Word revives my soul to action and equips me to be victorious in every situation."

"I decree that I am a lover of Your Word."

"Your Word causes me to hear more clearly, thus increasing my faith to apprehend all that You have for me."

"Your Word lights a path for my future and brings clarity to every turning point in my life."

"Your Word is the sword in my mouth that releases power in my life and in the lives of those I love."

Prayer:

"Lord, thank You for Your Word. Your Word truly revives my soul and speaks for every promise that You have made to me. Amen."

15

SAINT, NOT SINNER

What God Says About You:

He has rescued us completely from the tyrannical rule of darkness and has translated us into the kingdom realm of his beloved Son. For in the Son all our sins are canceled and we have the release of redemption through his very blood (Colossians 1:13-14 TPT).

Author's Note:

Have you ever heard the statement, "We are sinners saved by grace?" I have, but would like to propose to you the statement theologically is incorrect. Paul the apostle, when writing his letters to different churches, never addressed the church as "sinners." Paul addresses the church as "saints." Paul knew that the perfect sacrifice, Jesus Christ, makes all things new. When we receive Christ, our old life has been done away with and our new life has begun! The blood of Jesus makes us saints! We are no longer sinners! That is good news! Now activate this truth by speaking these declarations over your life!

Declarations:

Romans 8:1, Colossians 1:13-14,
Romans 6:11, Hebrews 9:1-28

"I am washed in the blood of Jesus; therefore, I am dead to sin and alive to live victoriously in Christ!"

> "I am *not* a sinner saved by grace,
> but a saint empowered by grace."

"I say to guilt, shame, and condemnation, 'Back off in Jesus' name!'"

"I am a new creation in Christ Jesus my Lord!"

"I declare over my body, soul, and spirit that my sins have been canceled forever because of the shed blood of Jesus!"

"The effects of sin and darkness have no authority over me because I have been translated into the kingdom of light!"

Prayer:

"Lord, thank You so much for dying in my place and cancelling my every sin. Thank You that I now stand here righteous because of what You did for me. I love You, Jesus. Amen."

16

SUPERNATURAL PROTECTION

What God Says About You:

He who dwells in the secret place of the Most High shall abide under the shadow of the Almighty (Psalm 91:1).

You will never worry about an attack of demonic forces at night nor have to fear a spirit of darkness coming against you. Don't fear a thing! (Psalm 91:5-6 TPT)

When we live our lives within the shadow of God Most High, our secret hiding place, we will always be shielded from harm. How then could evil prevail against us or disease infect us? God sends angels with special orders to protect you

wherever you go, defending you from all harm
(Psalm 91:9-11 TPT).

Author's Note:

We have some good news! You have supernatural protection from God! He sends angels to watch over you and your family! Now activate this truth by speaking these declarations over your life. Much Love!

Declarations:

Psalm 91, Psalm 27, Psalm 23, Exodus 14:19

"Every attack the enemy has sent my way is being stopped right now through angelic protection in Jesus' name!"

> "I live under supernatural protection because I abide under the shadow of God almighty!"

"I decree the Lord is my secret hiding place; therefore, I cannot be harmed by demonic forces."

"Accusation, slander, curses, loss, and disease cannot defeat me because the Lord is with me!"

Prayer:

> "Lord, thank You that You have become my hiding place. Being next to You gives me assurance that I am safe and secure in Jesus' name. Amen."

17

DIVINE FAVOR

What God Says About Me:

O Lord our God, let your sweet beauty rest upon us (Psalm 90:17 TPT).

My son, do not forget my law, but let your heart keep my commands; for length of days and long life and peace they will add to you. Let not mercy and truth forsake you; bind them around your neck, write them on the tablet of your heart, and so find favor and high esteem in the sight of God and man (Proverbs 3:1-4).

Author's Note:

When someone has favor with God, you can bet they will automatically have favor with man. Favor opens doors of destiny and promotion that propel us forward. Get ready for an upgrade of favor! Now activate this truth by speaking these declarations over your life. Much Love!

Declarations:

Psalm 90:17, Proverbs 3:1-4,
Psalm 67:1, Numbers 6:25

"I have favor with God and man."

"The favor in my life opens new doors and attracts divine opportunities that propel me forward."

"I declare that favor follows me everywhere I go."

"I declare that promotion, increase, and advancement are consistent in my life because of God's face shining on my ways."

"Every detail of my life is clothed with favor resulting in exponential increase."

Prayer:

Lord, thank You for the favor of Your face. When I have favor with You, it releases favor with man. Every good and perfect gift comes from You. Thank You so much for blessing me with Your precious favor. Amen."

18

VICTORIOUS LIVING

What God Says About Me:

Now thanks be to God who always leads us in triumph in Christ, and through us diffuses the fragrance of His knowledge in every place (2 Corinthians 2:14).

And the Lord said to Joshua, "Do not fear them, for I have delivered them into your hand" (Joshua 10:8).

The horse is prepared for the day of battle, but deliverance is of the Lord (Proverbs 21:31).

For the Lord alone is my Savior. What a feast of favor and bliss he gives his people! (Psalm 3:8 TPT)

Author's Note:

Did you know that God never leads you to a place where you will fail? When God leads us, the result will always be victory! His grace and love over your life set you up to be victorious in every situation! Now activate this truth by speaking these declarations over your life. Much Love!

Declarations:

2 Corinthians 2:14, Joshua 10:8,
Proverbs 21:31, Psalm 3:8

"I am wearing today's perfume of victory!"

"Like Jesus, I am victorious."

"I talk and act like a winner because I am a winner!"

"I declare, since God is on my side, nothing can stand in my way to victory!"

> "When others get around me, they smell the fragrance of victory and are inspired to step into victory with me!"

"Every enemy that tries to stop me, hinder me, or crush me will be defeated because God has delivered them into my hand!"

Prayer:

"Lord, thank You that the shed blood of Jesus makes me victorious in every situation. Because You are on my side, I cannot be defeated. Amen."

19

POWER OF THE
RENEWED MIND

What God Says About You:

And do not be conformed to this world, but be transformed by the renewing of your mind, that you may prove what is that good and acceptable and perfect will of God (Romans 12:2).

For "who has known the mind of the Lord that he may instruct Him?" But we have the mind of Christ (1 Corinthians 2:16).

Author's Note:

As believers, we have become spiritual gatekeepers of what comes in and what goes out of our lives. When our mind is renewed according to God's Word, we become in perfect alignment with God to prove His will on the earth. Our minds are a gate to the spirit realm that has the power to transform us. Transformation power is coming your way! Now activate this truth by speaking these declarations over your life. Much Love!

Declarations:

Romans 12:2, 1 Corinthians 2:16,
Isaiah 55:8-9, 2 Corinthians 10:5

"My mind is being transformed to prove the perfect will of God on the earth."

"I share head space with God, and He downloads His thoughts to me by the Holy Spirit, bringing kingdom solutions for me and others."

"I take every thought captive that tries to exalt itself above the life of Jesus in me."

"When I see an impossible situation, my mind gets supernatural downloads from the Holy Spirit that bring about breakthrough solutions."

"My mind is being rewired according to the mind of the spirit, putting me on the same page with heaven's perspective."

"My transformed mind gets creative ideas full of wisdom and knowledge to promote kingdom advancement."

Prayer:

"Thank You, Lord, for giving me a renewed mind to see like You see and think like You think. It is my honor and privilege to prove Your perfect will on earth. Amen."

20

BREAKING CURSES

What God Says About You:

For I, the Lord your God, am a jealous God, visiting the iniquity of the fathers upon the children to the third and fourth generations of those who hate Me, but showing mercy to thousands, to those who love Me and keep My commandments (Exodus 20:5-6).

Therefore, if anyone is in Christ, he is a new creation; old things have passed away; behold, all things have become new (2 Corinthians 5:17).

Author's Note:

These beautiful passages above give us a lot of truth concerning generational curses. The good news is, because we love God and are living in Christ now, we are not subject to any curse! Jesus dealt with every past, present, and future curse once and for all! No generational curse has power over you! Now activate this truth by speaking these declarations over your life. Much Love!

Declarations:

Exodus 20:5, Numbers 14:18,
Deuteronomy 24:16, Galatians 3:13,
2 Corinthians 5:17, 1 John 4:13

"I declare that because I love God, curses have no hold on me or my family."

"I am not subject to any curse because I am living in Christ."

"Christ has fully redeemed me and my family from every generational curse; therefore, I will not buy into the lie that curses can affect me."

> "I decree that every curse has been broken over me because of the blood of Jesus. I have been divinely set up for generational blessing!"

"I decree that every generational curse has forever been destroyed off me and my family legacy in Jesus' name!"

Prayer:

"Lord, thank You for the finished work of the cross. Thank You that only blessing has become my inheritance, not curses. Because I live in You and You in me, I can never be subject to any curse. Because of You, Lord, even my family has been divinely set up for generational blessing. I love You. Amen."

21

HEARING GOD'S VOICE

What God Says About You:

My own sheep will hear my voice and I know each one, and they will follow me (John 10:27 TPT).

However, when He, the Spirit of truth, has come, He will guide you into all truth; for He will not speak on His own authority, but whatever He hears He will speak; and He will tell you things to come (John 16:13).

Author's Note:

Did you know that you can hear God's voice? In fact, by nature you were designed to hear. We hear more than most of us realize. The issue is not in our inability to hear but in learning to recognize His voice when He speaks. We pray, as you declare these truths over your life today, that you would be awakened to recognize God's voice at a whole new level. Now activate the truth of God's Word by speaking these declarations over your life. Much Love!

Declarations:

John 10:27, John 16:13, Deuteronomy 4:36,
Book of Acts and epistles of Paul

"I was designed to hear God speak."

"When God speaks, I become fully aware and attentive knowing His desires and plan for me."

"I have eyes to see and ears to hear what the Spirit is saying to me."

"I hear God's voice through His Word, dreams, visions, prophecy, impressions, and heavenly encounters."

"I hear God's voice for others and act quickly to release it as God allows."

"My senses are trained and activated to hear God's voice when He speaks."

"Today I invite Your voice to guide and direct me."

Prayer:

Lord, thank You that You engineered me to hear Your voice. Thank You for blessing me with the gift of hearing. I position my heart today to listen when You speak. Amen."

22

MATTERS OF
THE HEART

What God Says About You:

*So above all, guard the affections of your heart,
for they affect all that you are. Pay attention to
the welfare of your innermost being, for from
there flows the wellspring of life* (Proverbs 4:23
TPT).

*A joyful heart is good medicine, but a crushed
spirit dries up the bones* (Proverbs 17:22 ESV).

*I have stored up your word in my heart, that
I might not sin against you* (Psalm 119:11
ESV).

Author's Note:

The genesis of true transformation starts with the affection of our hearts. The issues of life flow from the seat of our heart and need to be protected. The way we do life with God, others, and the world flows from this one thing. We must protect the most valuable part of who we are—our heart. Now activate the truth of God's Word by speaking these declarations over your life. Much Love!

Declarations:

Psalm 19:14, Proverbs 3:5-6, Philippians 4:7,
Matthew 5:8, Proverbs 4:23, Proverbs 17:22,
Mark 12:30, Psalm 119:11

> "My heart is the resting place of affection for King Jesus."

"I decree that my heart is filled with overflowing joy that brings divine health to my body."

"I declare that my entire being is filled with the light and life of God because of my love for the Lord Most High!"

"Your Word fills my heart in every way, reviving my soul!"

"I declare that my heart is a gate for the King of Glory to come through!"

Prayer:

"Lord, thank You that You have filled my heart with joy! The affections of my heart and the meditations of my mind shall be stayed on You. I love You. Amen."

23

RADICAL GENEROSITY

What God Says About You:

Give generously and generous gifts will be given back to you, shaken down to make room for more. Abundant gifts will pour out upon you with such an overflowing measure that it will run over the top! The measurement of your generosity becomes the measurement of your return (Luke 6:38 TPT).

Whoever is generous to the poor lends to the Lord, and he will repay him for his deed (Proverbs 19:17 ESV).

Let giving flow from your heart, not from a sense of religious duty. Let it spring up freely from the joy of giving—all because God loves hilarious generosity! (2 Corinthians 9:7 TPT)

Author's Note:

One of the characteristics of God the Father is that He is extravagantly generous. Our assignment in life is to beautifully reflect His nature to the world around us. Let's step into a life of extravagant generosity! Now activate the truth of God's Word by speaking these declarations over your life. Much Love!

Declarations:

Luke 6:38, Proverbs 19:17, 2 Corinthians 9:7-11

"I decree that I am a generous giver who gladly sows into the Kingdom of God."

"I don't give out of religious duty, but I give my time, money, and resources from a heart of abundance."

"Like Jesus, I am an extravagant giver!"

"I am generous; therefore, God can entrust me with more."

"Everything to which I put my hands turns into something good and is multiplied because generosity flows in me and through me."

Prayer:

"Lord, thank You that when I came to Christ, I became a partaker of Your divine nature. I am so thankful generosity flows through me as an expression of Your goodness to me and others. Amen."

24

Keep the Fire Burning

What God Says About You:

And the fire on the altar shall be kept burning on it; it shall not be put out (Leviticus 6:12).

Never restrain or put out the fire of the Holy Spirit (1 Thessalonians 5:19 TPT).

His word was in my heart like a burning fire shut up in my bones (Jeremiah 20:9).

Author's Note:

The Bible teaches us that we are kings and priests. Part of the job of an Old Testament priest was to keep the fire burning on the altar. Our job as New Testament priests is to keep the fire of the Holy Spirit burning on the altar of our hearts. This most precious flame represents our personal fellowship and love for the Holy Spirit. This precious fire must never go out. Let's keep it burning! Now activate the truth of God's Word by speaking these declarations over your life. Much Love!

Declarations:

Jeremiah 20:9, Leviticus 6:12,
1 Thessalonians 5:16-19, Luke 24:32

"As a worshiper of the Lord Jesus, I declare that the passion of my heart will be kept burning with a fire that cannot be contained."

> "I declare that because I live in constant joy, passionate prayer, and heartfelt thanksgiving, the fire of the Holy Spirit burns in me hotter and brighter every day."

"My love and passion for the Lord releases in me a fire that cannot be contained."

"I declare that God's Word is like a fire shut up in my bones."

"Like Jesus, my life and my words cause people to burn for more of God."

Prayer:

> "Lord Jesus, thank You for putting in me a burning heart. May the fire of Your Holy Spirit in me be kept burning always for Your glory. Amen."

KINGDOM WARFARE

What God Says About You:

For the weapons of our warfare are not carnal but mighty in God for pulling down strongholds, casting down arguments and every high thing that exalts itself against the knowledge of God, bringing every thought into captivity to the obedience of Christ (2 Corinthians 10:3-5).

He raised us up with Christ the exalted One, and we ascended with him into the glorious perfection and authority of the heavenly realm, for we are now co-seated as one with Christ! (Ephesians 2:6 TPT)

Author's Note:

Did you know that you are co-seated with Christ? We are called to war against our enemies from heaven to earth, not from earth toward heaven. We have an aerial view! We have a victory perspective! Because we are sitting next to Him, He speaks to our hearts and gives us words to declare that bring about kingdom victory! Now activate the truth of God's Word by speaking these declarations over your life. Much Love!

Declarations:

Ephesians 6, Ephesians 1:19-22,
2 Corinthians 10:3-5, Ephesians 2:6, Colossians 1

"God is on my side; therefore, I cannot be defeated in Jesus' name!"

"I am seated with Christ in heavenly places; therefore, I say to anxiety, fear, torment, heaviness, and depression to get under my feet in Jesus' name!"

"I am co-seated with Christ far above every seat of power, realm of government, principality, and authority in the heavenly realm."

"I declare that strongholds are pulled down and dismantled because my mind has been renewed to take captive lies from the enemy."

> "I command my soul to never be impressed by what the enemy is doing. Today I refine my focus to see and hear the good things that God is doing."

Prayer:

"Lord, thank You that my weapons are mighty in God! You have equipped me for every good work. Thank You for giving me the victory! Amen."

26

BEING A GLORY CARRIER

What God Says About You:

And he said, "Please, show me Your glory."
Then He said, "I will make all My goodness pass
before you, and I will proclaim the name of the
Lord before you" (Exodus 33:18-19).

And believers were increasingly added to the
Lord, multitudes of both men and women, so
that they brought the sick out into the streets
and laid them on beds and couches, that at
least the shadow of Peter passing by might fall
on some of them (Acts 5:14-15).

While Peter was speaking, the Holy Spirit cas-
caded over all those listening to his message
(Acts 10:44 TPT).

Author's Note:

In the Old Testament, the "Ark of Presence" was to be carried upon the shoulders of the priests. Everywhere the priests walked, the glory of God went with them. Because of Jesus, we have become New Testament priests who carry the Manifest Presence of God in the earth! Now activate the truth of God's Word by speaking these declarations over your life. Much Love!

Declarations:

Acts 19:11, Acts 10:44, Acts 5:14-15,
2 Chronicles 5:13-14, Exodus 33

"I decree that I am a glory carrier who carries the Manifest Presence of God."

> "The Manifest Presence of God is in me and on me; therefore, when people come into my atmosphere, they get healed, saved, and delivered by God's miracle power."

"I declare there is so much of God's glory in me that even my clothes are saturated with miracle power."

"Like Peter, when I speak, people come under the influence of the Holy Spirit's cascading presence."

"I declare that my family, friends, and community benefit from the Manifest Presence of God on my life."

Prayer:

"Lord, thank You for Your precious glory. Thank You that You chose me to carry Your glory. May Your Manifest Presence in my life always bring glory and honor to Jesus. Amen."

27

Refreshed by Love

What God Says About You:

I love each of you with the same love that the Father loves me. You must continually let my love nourish your hearts. If you keep my commands, you will live in my love, just as I have kept my Father's commands, for I continually live nourished and empowered by his love (John 15:9-10 TPT).

Now hope does not disappoint, because the love of God has been poured out in our hearts by the Holy Spirit who was given to us (Romans 5:5).

Author's Note:

Did you know that Jesus demonstrated His love for you when He died on the cross? His death and resurrection prove His love for you. You have permission to be refreshed by His love daily! Now activate this truth by speaking these declarations over your life!

Declarations:

John 15, 1 John 4:7-9, Romans 5:5, 1 Corinthians 13, 1 Peter 4:8, Ephesians 3:16-17, 1 John 3

"I declare over my heart, because of what Jesus did for me on the cross, I am worthy to receive all of God's love."

"I speak to my body, soul, and spirit saying, 'You are a temple of the Holy Spirit who is being filled daily with God's immense love.'"

"As I turn my affections to the Lord, I choose today to be nourished and saturated by the overwhelming presence of God's love for me."

"Because I am loved by God, I will release this contagious love to my family, friends, community, and to the world in Jesus' name."

"I declare that every gift of the Holy Spirit in me is expressed and energized by divine love."

> "I declare that my life is a love letter written by God to a lost and dying world."

Prayer:

"Lord Jesus, thank You that You proved Your love for me by dying in my place. I give You permission to refresh me with Your love throughout my day. Amen."

28

THIRST FOR
HOLY SPIRIT

What God Says About You:

O God of my life, I'm lovesick for you in this weary wilderness. I thirst with the deepest longings to love you more, with cravings in my heart that can't be described. Such yearning grips my soul for you, my God! I'm energized every time I enter your heavenly sanctuary to seek more of your power and drink in more of your glory. For your tender mercies mean more to me than life itself. How I love and praise you, God! Daily I will worship you passionately and with all my heart (Psalm 63:1-4 TPT).

Author's Note:

The highest privilege you and I have is fellowship with the Holy Spirit. When we have daily communion with Him, our thirst is quenched and we are completely satisfied. Now activate the truth of God's Word by speaking these declarations over your life. Much Love!

Declarations:

Psalm 16, Psalm 23, Psalm 63:1-8, John 14:15-17, 1 Corinthians 6:17 John 7

"I declare that I will always hunger and thirst for more of You, Holy Spirit."

"As I seek the Holy Spirit in the morning, my body, soul, and spirit are energized in Your presence."

> "My privileged habit is to worship and praise the Lord daily. My life is a 24-hour house of praise!"

"The anointing of the Lord's presence satisfies my soul like nothing else!"

"As I lie down at night, I will meditate and remember all that the Lord has done for me."

"Because the Holy Spirit satisfies my thirst, I will walk with songs of praise in my mouth throughout this day."

Prayer:

> "Lord, thank You that Your precious Holy Spirit satisfies my hunger and quenches my thirst. Thank You for giving me the most precious gift, Your Holy Spirit. Amen."

29

UNSHAKABLE FAITH

What God Says About You:

Jesus replied, "Let the faith of God be in you! Listen to the truth I speak to you: Whoever says to this mountain with great faith and does not doubt, 'Mountain, be lifted up and thrown into the midst of the sea,' and believes that what he says will happen, it will be done" (Mark 11:22-24 TPT).

Now faith is the substance of things hoped for, the evidence of things not seen (Hebrews 11:1).

Author's Note:

Faith is the heavenly substance that causes the unseen reality to become a seen reality. We all have been given a measure of faith. And this measure of faith can grow exponentially as we use the measure of faith we currently have. Let's begin to use the measure we have by making bold declarations today! Now activate the truth of God's Word by speaking these declarations over your life. Much Love!

Declarations:

Luke 22:32, Mark 11, Hebrew 11,
Matthew 21:22, Romans 10:17,
2 Corinthians 5:7, Philippians 4:13

"I declare I have great faith that brokers the dominion of God into inferior situations."

"Because Jesus has made intercession for me, my faith cannot be shaken."

> "My faith carries the substance of heaven that brings every dream, every promise, and every prayer request into my possession in Jesus' name!"

"I declare that I have faith to see impossible situations bend their knee to the name of Jesus."

"My faith is strengthened daily by the Holy Spirit's power!"

Prayer:

"Lord, thank You for the gift of faith. Thank You for praying for me that my faith will never fail. I love You, Jesus. Amen."

30

RELATIONSHIPS
THAT PROSPER

What God Says About You:

*With tender humility and quiet patience,
always demonstrate gentleness and generous
love toward one another, especially toward
those who may try your patience. Be faithful
to guard the sweet harmony of the Holy Spirit
among you in the bonds of peace, being one body
and one spirit, as you were all called into the
same glorious hope of divine destiny* (Ephesians
4:2-4 TPT).

Author's Note:

A sign of personal revival takes place when it affects every area of our lives, including relationships. God has designed us to have connection with Him and others. Relational connection with others is something God knows will help us grow and flourish. Covenant relationships are gifts from God that can also help us step into the fullness of our destiny and dreams. Now activate the truth of God's Word by speaking these declarations over your life. Much Love!

Declarations:

John 13:34, Ephesians 4:29, Colossians 3:19,
1 Thessalonians 5:11, 1 Peter 4:8, James 1:19-20

"I decree that I prosper in all of my relationships."

"I am quick to listen and slow to speak; therefore, my friends, family, and community trust me."

"I am a master encourager who brings words of hope and strength to my family, friends, and those I meet."

"My love for people is endless; therefore, I am quick to forgive those who hurt me or those who might offend me. The love of God in me causes me to live unoffendable."

> "My relationships with my family, friends, and loved ones will always succeed no matter what we may face."

Prayer:

"Lord, thank You for all the relationships You have blessed me with. Thank You for pouring out Your love in my heart. I am ready to love like You love and give like You give in Jesus' name. Amen."

31

WALKING
IN AUTHORITY

What God Says About You:

Jesus summoned together his twelve apostles and imparted to them authority over every demon and the power to heal every disease. Then he commissioned them to proclaim God's kingdom and to heal the sick to demonstrate that the kingdom had arrived (Luke 9:1-2 TPT).

Now you understand that I have imparted to you my authority to trample over his kingdom. You will trample upon every demon before you and overcome every power Satan possesses. Absolutely nothing will harm you as you walk in this authority (Luke 10:19 TPT).

Author's Note:

As Christians, we have been given access to a greater kingdom realm. Jesus has given us the ability to walk in His authority and power on the earth. Therefore, we can bring positive change to the world. This is your inheritance as a son and daughter of God Almighty! Now activate the truth of God's Word by speaking these declarations over your life. Much Love!

Declarations:

Joshua 1:3, Matthew 28:18-20, Luke 9:1-2,
Luke 10:19, Romans 8:17-18

"I have the ability to bring positive change to the world around me."

> "I can advance the kingdom of God without any fear of attacks in my life because God is with me."

"Wherever I go, I shift the atmosphere with the Kingdom of God."

"I have authority over every demon and any kind of darkness."

"I have the power to heal every disease."

"I heal the sick to demonstrate God's kingdom is here on the earth."

Prayer:

> "Jesus, thank You for the price You paid on the cross so that I can walk in Your authority. I believe that You are close to me and my loved ones all the time. I receive Your protection as I expand Your kingdom on the earth."

32

GROWING IN WISDOM

What God Says About You:

The Lord laid the earth's foundations with wisdom's blueprints. By his living-understanding all the universe came into being (Proverbs 3:19 TPT).

My goal is that they may be encouraged in heart and united in love, so that they may have the full riches of complete understanding, in order that they may know the mystery of God, namely, Christ, in whom are hidden all the treasures of wisdom and knowledge (Colossians 2:2-3 NIV).

If any of you lacks wisdom, you should ask God, who gives generously to all without finding fault, and it will be given to you (James 1:5 NIV).

The one who gets wisdom loves life; the one who cherishes understanding will soon prosper (Proverbs 19:8 NIV).

Author's Note

Through Christ, we have access to the treasures of wisdom and knowledge. As we grow in intimacy with Him, we will begin to receive revelation and insight through the Holy Spirit. Wisdom is a gift of the Holy Spirit that imparts understanding, strategy, advice, and insight that only God can give. Now activate the truth of God's Word by speaking these declarations over your life. Much Love!

Declarations:

1 Corinthians 12:8, James 1:5,
2 Chronicles 2:1-18, 1 Kings 3:7-15

"God has given me the ability to make the right decisions."

"I have creative solutions within me. I am a solutionist."

"I bring creative strategies to situations."

> "God's wisdom gives me the ability to build and design my life with excellence."

Prayer

"Heavenly Father, thank You for generously giving me Your wisdom when I ask. I make a commitment today to keep my eyes, efforts, and heart focused on You. I believe that You will share Your heart and perfect ways with me."

33

LEADING WITH INFLUENCE

What God Says About You:

If you want to be my disciple, follow me and you will go where I am going. And if you truly follow me as my disciple, the Father will shower his favor upon your life (John 12:26 TPT).

As Jesus grew, so did his wisdom and maturity. The favor of men increased upon his life, for he was loved greatly by God (Luke 2:52 TPT).

Author's Note

As sons and daughters, we have favor with God and man. We have a perfect heavenly Father whose leadership is good for us. As we follow his ways, favor and influence will follow. When we know we are accepted by the Father, we will not go looking for people's approval, which usually produces unhealthy performance and cheap networking. Rest in God's goodness today. Now activate the truth of God's Word by saying the following declarations over your life. Much Love!

Declarations:

Psalm 5:12, Psalm 90:17, John 12:19,26,
Luke 2:52, Isaiah 55:5, Isaiah 22:22

"God gives me favor and influence."

> "Because I have favor with God, nothing can stop me."

"My leadership will impact nations."

"I have favor with people and opportunities that are best for me."

"God opens doors for me that no one can shut."

"I lead with service and encouragement."

Prayer

"Father, thank You for pouring out Your favor upon my life. Thank You for removing every obstacle from my path as I commit to follow You. I believe that You are a good Father and will bring the best opportunities my way."

34

HOLY INTOXICATION

What God Says About You:

And don't get drunk with wine, which is rebellion; instead be filled continually with the Holy Spirit. And your hearts will overflow with a joyful song to the Lord. Keep speaking to each other with words of Scripture, singing the Psalms with praises and spontaneous songs given by the Spirit! (Ephesians 5:18-19 TPT)

These people are not drunk like you think they are, for it is only nine o'clock in the morning. This is the fulfillment of what was prophesied through the prophet Joel, for God says: "This is what I will do in the last days—I will pour out my Spirit on everybody and cause your sons and

*daughters to prophesy, and your young men will
see visions, and your old men will experience
dreams from God. The Holy Spirit will come
upon all my servants, men and women alike,
and they will prophesy"* (Acts 2:15-18 TPT).

Author's Note:

In his letter to the church in Ephesus, Paul is trying
to describe what being filled with the Spirit is like. As
he gives the church the charge to be filled with the Holy
Spirit, he compares that experience with being intoxicated with earthly wine. The word *intoxicated* means to
be under the influence of something. Paul was saying that
we are not to let anything in this world influence our lives
but the intoxicating presence of the Holy Spirit. When
you get immersed in the fire of the Holy Spirit, something
is transferred from God's heart into yours! On the day
of Pentecost, those who were being filled with the Holy
Spirit were accused of drinking too much wine. Many
times, when God fills us to overflowing our whole being,
which includes body, soul, and spirit, becomes completely
intoxicated by God, causing a deep change in us. When

God fills our mind, will, and emotions, we become filled with righteousness, peace, and joy! We become transformed by God's glory! Now activate this truth by speaking these declarations over your life. Much Love!

Declarations:

Acts 2, Ephesians 5:18-19, 2 Corinthians 5:13,
Galatians, Acts 4, Acts 13:52,
Proverbs 31:25, Psalm 92:10

"The Holy Spirit has filled me with the oil of joy and laughter that releases healing and strength to me."

"I declare that my body, soul, and spirit are under the influence of the Holy Spirit."

"Today, I give God permission to intoxicate me with the Holy Spirit, filling me with righteousness, peace, and joy!"

Prayer:

"Lord, You paid a price for me to be filled and flooded with Your Holy Spirit. Fill me to overflowing. Have Your way with me. Amen."

35

WORDS OF LIFE

What God Says About You:

Simon Peter replied, "Lord, to whom would we go? You have the words that give eternal life" (John 6:68 NLT).

But if you live in life-union with me and if my words live powerfully within you—then you can ask whatever you desire and it will be done (John 15:7 TPT).

So also will be the word that I speak; it does not return to me unfulfilled. My word performs my purpose and fulfills the mission I sent it out to accomplish (Isaiah 55:11 TPT).

Then God said, "Let there be light," and there was light (Genesis 1:3 NLT).

Author's Note:

The Bible exists by the *Word* of God, and everything exists from His spoken word (see John 1:1-3). Jesus' words carry life because He is life. Throughout scripture, we can observe that words matter. Being united with Christ includes being connected with His written and spoken word daily. From this place of oneness with Christ, His life-giving words will be in us. When we speak what He says, we co-labor with Him to create life, hope, and miracles into situations. Now activate the truth of God's Word by saying these declarations over your life. Much Love!

Declarations:

John 12:9-12, John 15, Genesis 1, John 1,
Proverbs 18:21, Isaiah 55:11,
Matthew 21:21, Hebrews 1:3

"I create with my words."

"When I speak God's Word, chaos comes into order."

"My words create miracles that glorify Jesus."

"My words contain life-giving power."

"My words navigate my life; therefore, I choose to speak words that positively change the course of my life."

"The Father's words over me are kind, gentle, and forgiving of my mistakes; now, I give those same words to others."

Prayer:

"Heavenly Father, thank You for sending Jesus, who is Your living Word. Help me to remain in life-union with You. Holy Spirit, fill me with the love, the power, and the words of Jesus. Fill my mouth with words that bring life to myself, my family, and my loved ones. I believe that You will transform me with Your words toward me. Thank You for Your merciful words that birth miracles. Amen."

36

LIVING LIKE JESUS

What God Says About You:

The Son is the dazzling radiance of God's splendor, the exact expression of God's true nature—his mirror image! He holds the universe together and expands it by the mighty power of his spoken word. He accomplished for us the complete cleansing of sins, and then took his seat on the highest throne at the right hand of the majestic One (Hebrews 1:3 TPT).

By living in God, love has been brought to its full expression in us so that we may fearlessly face the day of judgment, because all that Jesus now is, so are we in this world (1 John 4:17 TPT).

I want you to pattern your lives after me, just as I pattern mine after Christ (1 Corinthians 11:1 TPT).

Author's Notes:

Living like Jesus is more than a smile and a good mood. Living like Jesus is living a life of the miraculous that serves humanity. It is living a life that brings glory to the Father! When we read transformation stories in the Bible, His Word promises that we have permission to do the same. Jesus fulfills the will of God. Doing what Jesus did here on earth mirrors God's will (see Hebrews 1:3). Everything that Jesus is *now* is what we have access to be on this earth. Now activate the truth of God's Word by saying these declarations over your life. Much Love!

Declarations:

John 15, John 17:10, Acts 10:38,
Mark 16:17-18, Romans 8:11, Romans 8:17

"All that Jesus did on this earth, I can do because He lives in me!"

"Jesus is my perfect example, and I have the power of the Holy Spirit to help me live like Him."

"God gives me creative ways to do good for others."

"My actions transform the world around me."

> "I have the *same* Spirit of Jesus; therefore, I can expect to have miracles, signs, and wonders follow me."

Prayer:

"Jesus, thank You for going to the cross for me so that I could have all that is Yours. I give You my past with all its failures and disappointments. I ask that You fill me with the *same* Spirit that brings resurrection life. Holy Spirit, I need You to live a life like Jesus. Amen."

37

JESUS MAKES
ME ENOUGH

What God Says About You:

She gives out revelation-truth to feed others. She is like a trading ship bringing divine supplies from the merchant (Proverbs 31:14 TPT).

Never doubt God's mighty power to work in you and accomplish all this. He will achieve infinitely more than your greatest request, your most unbelievable dream, and exceed your wildest imagination! He will outdo them all, for his miraculous power constantly energizes you (Ephesians 3:20 TPT).

And you did not receive the "spirit of religious duty," leading you back into the fear of never being good enough. But you have received the "Spirit of full acceptance," enfolding you into the family of God. And you will never feel orphaned, for as he rises up within us, our spirits join him in saying the words of tender affection, "Beloved Father!" (Romans 8:15 TPT).

Author's Notes:

Like many, I have had my fair share of overcoming feelings of inadequacy. The fear of not being enough blocks us from walking in abundant life. Jesus fills in all our gaps and makes our ordinary extraordinary! He desires to partner with us to fulfill our greatest dreams. Resting in the Father's acceptance is part of the adoption process. Let His love qualify you. Now activate the truth of God's Word by saying these declarations over your life. Much Love!

Declarations:

Romans 8:17, Romans 8:14-16, Proverbs 31:14,
Exodus 4:10-12, Amos 7, Judges 6:15,16

"I am capable, and I have what it takes to succeed."

"I don't wait for others to recognize my gifting before I act in faith."

"I am adopted and accepted by the heavenly Father."

> "God's love qualifies me."

"Jesus gives me revelation truth, and I bring miracles to others."

"Because of what Jesus paid for on the cross, I bring supernatural supplies from heaven."

Prayer:

"Father, thank You for adopting me into Your family. Thank You, Holy Spirit, for making God's fatherhood real to me. Father, I believe that You gave Your Son so I could inherit all Your treasures, including the greatest miracle of salvation. I believe I can bring miracles and truth to those in need. Today I give You my yes. Amen."

38

HOPE THAT TRANSFORMS

What God Says About You:

For this is the hope of our salvation. But hope means that we must trust and wait for what is still unseen. For why would we need to hope for something we already have? So, because our hope is set on what is yet to be seen, we patiently keep on waiting for its fulfillment (Romans 8:24-25 TPT).

Against all odds, when it looked hopeless, Abraham believed the promise and expected God to fulfill it. He took God at his word, and as a result he became the father of many nations. God's declaration over him came to pass: "Your descendants will be so many that they will be impossible to count!" (Romans 4:18 TPT)

Who has ever intimately known the mind of the Lord Yahweh well enough to become his counselor? Christ has, and we possess Christ's perceptions (1 Corinthians 2:16 TPT).

Author's Note:

When I use the word *hope*, sometimes I equate it with a "wish." But God's Word reminds me that His hope gives me patient anticipation of His goodness. No matter how long I have waited for a fulfilled promise, hope keeps me from quitting. My expectation of the future changes when my mind is set to hope. Studies have proven that how we think affects the choices we make. Choices determine our future. Some studies suggest that negative emotions can weaken the immune response. There is a strong link between positivity and health. Additional studies have found that a hopeful attitude improves outcomes and conditions in the body—specifically traumatic brain injury, stroke, and brain tumors. Now, activate God's truth by saying these declarations over your life. Much Love!

Declarations:

Romans 7:25, Romans 8:5-7, Romans 12:2, James 1:8

"I am transformed by changing the way I think."

"I am empowered to make the right choices for my life."

"The Holy Spirit enables me to discern God's will for my life."

"I have stable thoughts and make good choices."

"I choose to focus on the good in every situation."

"My renewed mind resets my body to receive life from the Spirit."

Prayer:

"Father, thank You for giving me a renewed mind in Christ Jesus. Holy Spirit, I ask You to transform me inwardly through a reformation of how I think. I give You any negative emotions, trauma, and toxicity in exchange for hope, healing, and joy. Amen."

39

Our Original Design

What God Says About You:

So we are convinced that every detail of our lives is continually woven together for good, for we are his lovers who have been called to fulfill his designed purpose (Romans 8:28 TPT).

Author's Notes:

I always enjoy a good superhero origin story. They usually include the back story on how the person developed into being "super." Their defining moment comes when they are faced with the decision to quit or to courageously fulfill their destiny. Remembering their identity ignites their inherent power that equips them for victory. This can be parabolic for our lives in many ways. My life changed when I discovered that my identity was not determined by my failures and shortcomings. My identity is in Christ, in whom all treasures are found. Because of the Spirit of Christ living in us, we are dead to sin and alive in Him (see Romans 8). When praying, I often ask Him to show me His original plan for the situation I need solutions for. I ask Him to show me His original design for people, nations, situations, etc. God's design will always include a beautiful tapestry that displays love and purpose. His heart for humanity was displayed when He gave His Son Jesus to die on the cross for us. Jesus is the only solution for sin's problems. Jesus is the divine reset button that provides a way for us to return to God's intent. He desires that we live in freedom and peace. If your current status does not reflect God's original plan for you, it doesn't mean He can't reset it. Now activate these truths by saying these declarations over your life. Much Love!

Declarations:

Romans 8, Colossians 1:12, Romans 8:17-18,
1 Peter 1:4, Colossians 1:12, Ephesians 2:13,
Ephesians 1:4, Psalm 139

> "From my mother's womb,
> I was designed for victory."

"Today I choose to walk into freedom and all the Father has for me."

"Jesus resets my life and my body by the power of the Holy Spirit."

"I am a co-heir with Christ and all that He has is available to me."

Prayer

"Thank You, Jesus, for resetting me to my original design. I receive Your Holy Spirit that enables me to fulfill my destiny. Today I choose to leave my past and walk into the freedom of my real identity—Your child. Amen."

40

ARISE AND SHINE

What God Says About You:

Arise, shine; for your light has come! And the glory of the Lord is risen upon you. For behold, the darkness shall cover the earth, and deep darkness the people; but the Lord will arise over you, and His glory will be seen upon you. The Gentiles shall come to your light, and kings to the brightness of your rising (Isaiah 60:1-3).

You are the light of the world. A city that is set on a hill cannot be hidden. Nor do they light a lamp and put it under a basket, but on a lamp-stand, and it gives light to all who are in the house. Let your light so shine before men, that they may see your good works and glorify your Father in heaven (Matthew 5:14-16).

Authors Note:

Did you know that you were created to shine brightly for the King of Glory? Jesus came as the light of the world, and then He passed the baton off to you and me, then said, "You are the light of the world" (Matthew 5:14). You and I have become the very image of the One and only Jesus Christ! We have become His exact representation! We are image bearers of light in the darkness! Now is the time for you to arise and shine to a lost and dying world! Now activate this truth by declaring these biblically based declarations over your life. Much Love to you!

Declarations:

Matthew 5:14-16, Isaiah 60, Matthew 10:7-8, Matthew 28, Acts 1:8, Mark 16:15, Hebrews 1:1-3, Colossians 1

"Today I will arise and shine, reflecting the beauty of Jesus everywhere I go."

"I am salt and light to the world. My life causes those around me to become hungry for God."

"My life is the express image of Jesus."

"The glory of God shall be seen upon me and nations shall come to the light that I carry."

Prayer:

"Lord Jesus, thank You for putting Your light and life in me. Help me to shine brightly and reflect Your beauty. I love You. Amen."

CLOSING
RECOMMENDATION

We hope you have enjoyed this 40-day devotional. We would like to encourage you to go through this devotional again to get the full benefit. Repetition is the mother of all skill. Here are three things that will help you daily, weekly, and monthly as you pursue total transformation.

1. Recite: Read allowed the scriptures and declarations daily, weekly, and monthly. "Faith comes by hearing, and hearing by the word of God" (Romans 10:17).

2. Remember: Think often of what you have read. Biblical meditation is key for renewing your

mind. "Oh, how I love your law! I meditate on it all day long" (Psalm 119:97 NIV).

3. Replay: Replay includes doing steps one and two over again until you see your thinking change and the reality of God's Word being made manifest in your life. "Be transformed by the renewing of your mind" (Romans 12:2).

BIBLIOGRAPHY

Ziglar, Zig and Ziglar, Tom (2018). *Born To Win: Find Your Success Code*. Ziglar Success Books.

Johnson, Bill (2005). *The Supernatural Power of a Transformed Mind: Access to a Life of Miracles*. Destiny Image.

Richter, Maria (2010). "Do Words Hurt?" Volume 148, Issue 2, pages 177-354. Sciencedirect.com.

About Tommy and Miriam Evans

Tommy and Miriam Evans travel locally, nationally, and internationally holding revival meetings, miracle services, and supernatural school intensives for inviting churches and conferences. Along with their itinerant ministry, Tommy and Miriam are senior leaders of Trinity Church's Saturday Night Awakening Service in Cedar Hill, Texas where they hold weekly revival meetings.

Tommy and Miriam have co-founded Mandate of Hope Ministries. Mandate of Hope is a global itinerant ministry organized to function on a local, national, and international scale by preaching and teaching the Gospel of Jesus Christ through the power of the Holy Spirit.

Along with their ministry, Miriam and Tommy serve as members of the Apostolic Council of Prophetic Elders with Generals International.

Tommy, Miriam, and their five children, Kathryn, Madison, Lauren, Benjamin, and Levi, live in the Dallas/Fort Worth, Texas area.